# Back to Beginnings

# BACK TO BEGINNINGS

*Reflections on the Tao*

## Huanchu Daoren

*Translated by* Thomas Cleary

SHAMBHALA
*Boston & London*
1998

Shambhala Publications, Inc.
Horticultural Hall
300 Massachusetts Avenue
Boston, Massachusetts 02115
*http://www.shambhala.com*

9  8  7  6  5  4  3  2  1

⊗ This edition is printed on acid-free paper that meets
the American National Standards Institute Z39.48 Standard.
Distributed in the United States by Random House, Inc.
in Canada by Random House of Canada Ltd.
and in the United Kingdom by the Random Century Group

The Library of Congress catalogues the previous edition
of this book as follows:

Hung, Tzu-ch'eng, fl. 1596.
  [Ts'ai ken t'an. English]
  Back to beginnings: reflections on the Tao/Huanchu Daoren;
translated by Thomas Cleary.—1st ed.
      p.  cm.   Translation of: Ts'ai ken t'an.
ISBN 0-87773-577-8 (alk. paper)
ISBN 1-57062-377-5 (Shambhala Centaur Editions)
I. Meditations.  2. Life.  I. Cleary, Thomas F., 1949–.
II. Title.  90-55071 BD430.H86  1990 CIP  181'.114—dc20

# Translator's Preface

*Back to Beginnings* is a collection of meditations on fundamental things in human life. It was written around 1600 by a retired Chinese scholar, Hong Yingming, whose Taoist name, Huanchu Daoren, means "A Wayfarer Back to Beginnings." In it can be seen a form of lay Taoism dating many centuries further back into history, in which the historical and sociological insights of pristine Confucianism were combined with the advanced educational and psychological knowledges and methodologies of Buddhism and Taoism.

Nothing is really known of Huanchu Daoren, except that he wrote the present volume of meditations, which was originally entitled "Vegetable Root Talks," and compiled a collection of stories on the extraordinary deeds of Taoist and Buddhist adepts. He identifies himself as a Confucian, which means that he is a layman; his Taoist epithet, "Back to Beginnings," says in calendrical symbolism that he has passed the age of sixty, has retired from public affairs, and has started a new cycle of life. These are his thoughts on the secrets of serenity and wisdom in a changing world, reflections on the four seasons of a lifetime.

*Back to Beginnings*

解籜

Those who live virtuously may be desolate for a time, but those who depend on flattering the powerful are destitute forever. Awakened people observe what is beyond things and think about life after death, so they would rather experience temporary desolation than permanent destitution.

When you are but slightly involved in the world, the effect the world has on you is also slight. When you are deeply enmeshed in affairs, your machinations also deepen. So for enlightened people simplicity is better than refinement, and freedom is better than punctiliousness.

The mentality of enlightened people, like the blue of the sky and the light of the sun, is not to be concealed from others. The talents of enlightened people, as gems to be hidden, are not to be easily made known to others.

People are considered pure of heart when they do not approach power and pomp; but those who can be near without being affected are the purest of all. People are considered high-minded when they do not know how to plot and contrive; but those who know how yet do not do so are the highest of all.

When you are constantly hearing offensive words and always have some irritating matter in mind, only then do you have a whetstone for character development. If you hear only what pleases you, and deal only with what thrills you, then you are burying your life in deadly poison.

Even the birds are sad in a violent storm; even the plants are happy on a sunny day. Obviously, heaven and earth cannot do without a moderating force for even a day; the human mind cannot do without a joyful spirit for even a day.

Strong drink, fat meat, and spicy dishes are not really flavorful; true flavor is delicate. Marvels and oddities are not characteristic of completed people; complete people are simply normal.

The universe is silent and unmoving, but the workings of energy never rest, even for a while. The sun and moon are in motion day and night, but their light never changes. So enlightened people should have a sense of urgency when at leisure and a mood of relaxation when they're busy.

Late at night, when everyone is quiet, sit alone and gaze into the mind; then you will notice illusion ending and reality appearing. You gain a great sense of potential in this every time. Once you have noticed reality appearing yet find that illusion is hard to escape, you also find yourself greatly humbled.

Blessings often give rise to injury, so be careful when things are going your way. Success may be achieved after failure, so don't just give up when you've been disappointed.

Those who live simply are often pure, while those who live luxuriously may be slavish and servile. It seems that the will is clarified by plainness, while conduct is ruined by indulgence.

Be open and broad-minded in this life, so that none may bear a complaint against you. Let your generosity continue long after your death, so that people may be satisfied.

Where the road is narrow, stop for a moment to let others pass; when there is good food, leave a third of your portion for others to enjoy. This is one good way to live in the world in peace and happiness.

There is a true Buddha in family life; there is a real Tao in everyday activities. If people can be sincere and harmonious, promoting communication with a cheerful demeanor and friendly words, that is much better than formal meditation practice.

People who are compulsively active are unstable, while those who are addicted to quietude are indifferent. One should have a lively spirit while in the midst of tranquillity; this is the mentality of the enlightened.

Don't be too severe in criticizing people's faults; consider how much they can bear. Don't be too lofty in enjoining virtue, so people may be able to follow.

A grub in filth is dirty, but it changes into a cicada and sips dew in the autumn breeze. Rotting plants have no luster, but they turn into foxfire and glow in the summer moonlight. So we know that purity emerges from impurity, and light is born from darkness.

Conceit and arrogance are acquired states of mind. Conquer acquired states of mind, and basic sanity can unfold. Passion and willfulness are part of false consciousness; erase false consciousness, and true consciousness will appear.

Think about food on a full stomach, and you find you don't care about taste. Think of lust after making love, and you find you don't care about sex. Therefore, if people always reflect on the regret they will feel afterward to forestall folly at the moment, they will be stable and will not err in action.

When in an important position, do not lose the mood of retirement in the countryside. When at leisure in retreat, keep the affairs of state in mind.

One need not necessarily seek success in the world; avoiding mistakes is itself a success.

Do not seek gratitude from other people; it is a favor not to be resented.

Conscientious diligence is a virtue, but if it is too harsh, it does not bring comfort and joy. Frugality and plainness are noble, but if they are too austere, there is no way to help others.

Those who have come to an impasse should examine their original intentions; those who have succeeded should note where they are heading.

When the rich and well-established, who should be generous, are instead spiteful and cruel, they make their behavior wretched and base in spite of their wealth and position. When the intellectually brilliant, who should be reserved, instead show off, they are ignorant and foolish in their weakness in spite of their brilliance.

After one has been in a lowly position, one knows how dangerous it is to climb to a high place. Once one has been in the dark, one knows how revealing it is to go into the light. Having maintained quietude, one knows how tiring compulsive activity is. Having nurtured silence, one knows how disturbing much talk is.

One can shed worldliness after putting down mundane ambitions. One can enter sagehood after putting down spiritual ambitions.

Desires do not hurt the mind as much as opinions do. The senses do not hinder enlightenment as much as the intellect does.

鯉

Human feelings are fickle; the world is full of hazards. When at an impasse, know how to step back. When things are going smoothly, strive to remain deferential.

In dealing with petty people, it is easy to be severe with them but hard to avoid despising them. In dealing with superior people, it is easy to be respectful to them but hard to be courteous to them.

It is better to be simple and reject intellectualism, to retain one's sanity and return it to the universe. It is better to decline extravagance and be content with plainness, to leave a good name in the world.

To conquer demons, first conquer your mind. When the mind is subdued, demons withdraw obediently. To control knaves, first control your own mood. When your mood is balanced, scoundrels cannot get at you.

Teaching students is like bringing up a chaste daughter; it is necessary to be strict about where they go and to be careful about who they see. Once they get in with the wrong people, it is like planting bad seed in a clear field; it will be hard to grow a good crop.

In matters of desire, don't get hastily involved because of easy availability; once you get involved, you will sink in deeply. In matters of principle, don't back off for fear of difficulty; once you back down, you will lose your ground entirely.

Those who are careful take good care of themselves and others as well, careful in every situation. Those who are careless slight themselves and others too, careless in everything. Enlightened people make it a point to be neither too concerned nor too indifferent.

To those who approach you with riches, respond with humanity. To those who approach you with rank, respond with justice. Enlightened people are not prisoners of rulers. When people are determined, they can overcome fate; when the will is unified, it can mobilize energy. Enlightened people do not even let nature put them in a set mold.

In establishing yourself in society, if you are without nobility of character, it will be like brushing your clothes in the dust or washing your feet in the mud. How can you be free? In your dealings with the world, if you are not deferential, it will be a moth flying into a flame or a ram butting a fence. How can you be at peace?

Students need to gather in their vital spirit and set it wholly on one path. If you cultivate personal qualities with your mind focused on success and honor, you will make no real progress. If you read with your interest focused on enjoyment of literary aesthetics, you will not deepen your mind.

There is great compassion in everyone; a Buddha and a butcher do not have different minds. There is real enjoyment everywhere, whether in a gilded mansion or in a reed hut. It is just that when one is shrouded by desires and locked up in feelings, one misses what is really there; and that makes all the difference in the world.

To develop strength of character and cultivate enlightenment require a degree of aloofness. Once there is fascination, you pursue objects of desire. To help the world or run a state requires a sense of detachment. Once there is attachment, you fall into danger.

Good people are calm not only in action; their spirits are gentle even in dreams. Bad people are perverse not only in their deeds; even their voices and laughter are vicious.

When the liver is diseased, the eyesight fails; when the kidneys are diseased, the hearing is adversely affected. The disease is not visible, but its effects are. Therefore, enlightened people, wishing to be free from obvious faults, first get rid of hidden faults.

There is no greater fortune than having few concerns, no greater misfortune than having many worries. Only those who have suffered over their concerns know the blessing of having few concerns. Only those who have calmed their minds know the misfortune of having many worries.

In an orderly era one should be punctilious; in a turbulent era one should be flexible. In a degenerate era one should combine punctiliousness and flexibility. In dealing with good people one should be magnanimous; in dealing with bad people one should be strict. In dealing with average people one should combine magnanimity and strictness.

Do not think about whatever service you may have done for others; think about what you may have done to offend them. Don't forget what others have done for you; forget what others have done to offend you.

When those who give charity do so without any sense of self-satisfaction and without any thought of reward, even a small gift is great. When those who aid others calculate their own sacrifice and demand gratitude and recompense, even a great gift is small.

People's circumstances may be settled or unsettled; how can you guarantee that you alone are settled? Your own feelings may be reasonable or unreasonable; how can you expect others to always be reasonable? It is useful to see things in this light and thereby correct the contradictions in your expectations for yourself and others.

Only when your mind is clean are you in a suitable state to read books and study the ancients. Otherwise, when you read of a good deed, you will try to claim it as your own; and when you hear a good saying, you will borrow it to cover your shortcomings. This is like lending weapons to a rebel, or giving supplies to a thief.

The extravagant who are rich yet unsatisfied are not as good as the frugal who have more than enough even though they be poor. The talented who work hard and become targets of resentment cannot compare with the inept who take it easy and keep their real nature whole.

Those who read books but do not see the wisdom of the sages are slaves of the letter.

Those in public office who do not love the people are thieves stealing salaries. Those who teach but do not themselves practice what they teach are mere talkers. Those who try to do successful work without considering development of character will find it insubstantial.

In the human mind there is a real book, but it is locked up in fragmentary editions. There is a real melody, but it is obscured by weird songs and ostentatious dances. Students should sweep away externals and directly seek the original; only then will they be really able to experience it and use it.

In the mind engaged in struggling with hardship, one always finds something delightful. The sorrow of disappointment arises in the complacency of satisfaction.

立圖

Wealth, status, honor, and praise that come from enlightened qualities are like flowers in the mountains, growing and blossoming naturally. Those that come from achievements in one's career are like flowers in pots, being moved about, removed, replanted. Those that are gained by temporal power are like flowers in vases, without roots, soon to wilt.

When spring comes and the weather warms, the flowers beautify the land and the birds chirp pleasantly. If people who are lucky enough to obtain official positions and be well fed and housed do not make it their concern to establish good education and do good works, even if they live a hundred years, it is as if they had never lived at all.

The learned should be vigorous and diligent, but they should also be free-spirited. If they are too rigorous and austere, they have the death-dealing quality of autumn but lack the life-giving quality of spring. How can they develop people then?

Those who are really virtuous have no reputation for virtue. Those who establish such a reputation do so for selfish motives. Those who are really skillful have no cunning artifices. Those who employ cunning artifice are inept because of it.

There is a kind of vessel that tips over when it is full. A piggy bank is not broken as long as it is empty. So for enlightened people it is better to dwell in nonbeing than in being, better to be lacking than replete.

As long as people have not gotten rid of the desire for fame, even if they scorn princehood and content themselves with poverty, they are still captives of the senses. As long as people have not shed impetuous adventurism, even if they help the nation, it is just an exploit.

If the mind is illumined, there is clear blue sky in a dark room. If the thoughts are muddled, there are malevolent ghosts in broad daylight.

People know that fame and position are pleasant, but they do not know that the pleasure of anonymity is most real. People know that hunger and cold are distressing, but they do not know that the distress of not experiencing cold or hunger is greater.

If you fear that people will know if you do something bad, then there is something good in bad. If you are eager for people to know when you do something good, then there is something bad in good.

The workings of heaven are unfathomable—sometimes encouraging, sometimes suppressing. All this makes sport of heroes and tumbles the great. Enlightened people take adversity in stride and are prepared for trouble even when at ease; therefore, they are not at the mercy of fate.

Those who are harsh and aggressive are like fire, burning whatever they touch. Those who are ungrateful are like ice, chilling whomever they encounter. Those who are obsessive and inflexible are like stagnant water or rotten wood, already void of life. All such people have trouble accomplishing works and extending welfare.

One should not seek happiness, just nurture the spirit of joy as the basis of summoning happiness. One should not try to escape misfortune, just get rid of viciousness as a means of avoiding misfortune.

If ninety percent of what you say hits the mark, you will not necessarily be praised as exceptional; but if one statement misses the mark, you will be blamed by everyone for this mistake. If nine out of ten plans work, you will not necessarily be considered successful; but when one plan fails, you will be heaped with abuse. Therefore enlightened people prefer silence to impetuosity and ineptitude to cleverness.

When the air is warm, there is growth; when it is cold, there is death. Similarly, those who are by nature cold receive little happiness, while those who are warm of heart are richly blessed.

The road of truth is broad; set the mind on it, and you feel expansive openness and broad clarity. The road of human desires is narrow; set foot on it, and you see brambles and mire before you.

Happiness lasts only for those who achieve it by using both hardship and ease as means of self-cultivation. Knowledge is real only in those who achieve it by investigation in which both doubt and faith play a part.

The mind should be emptied, for when it is emptied, truth comes to it. The mind should be fulfilled, for when it is fulfilled, desire for things doesn't enter it.

Soil with a lot of manure in it produces abundant crops; water that is too clear has no fish. Therefore, enlightened people should maintain the capacity to accept impurities and should not be solitary perfectionists.

Even a wild horse can be tamed; even metal that is difficult to work eventually goes into a mold. If you just take it easy and do not stir yourself, you will never make any progress. It has been said, "It is no disgrace to have many afflictions; I would worry if there never were any afflictions."

Even a little greed and selfishness turn strength into weakness, knowledge into ignorance, care into cruelty, and purity into defilement, thus ruining one's character. Therefore, people of old deemed freedom from greed precious, and this is how they got beyond the world.

The eyes and ears, seeing and hearing, are external plunderers; emotions, desires, and opinions are internal plunderers. But if the inner mind is awake and alert, sitting aloof in the middle of it all, then these plunderers change and become members of the household.

To count on success as yet unattained is not as good as preserving work already accomplished. To regret past mistakes is not as good as preventing future errors.

One should be high-minded, but not unrealistic; punctilious, but not picayune. Tastes should be simple, but not too austere; behavior should be strict and clear, but not too severe.

When the wind comes to sparse bamboo, the bamboo doesn't keep the sound after the wind has passed. When geese cross a cold pond, the pond doesn't retain their reflection after the geese have gone. Similarly, the minds of enlightened people become manifest when events occur and then become empty when the events are over.

Even if you do no work that is particularly lofty or far-reaching, if you can shed mundane feelings, that is a great achievement. Even if you do not strive much for progress in learning, if you can minimize the influence things have on you, you will soar into the realm of sages.

Be chivalrous in dealing with acquaintances; be pure of heart in being yourself.

Do not claim precedence over others for favor or gain; do not lag behind others in doing good works. Do not take more than your share; do not do less than your duty.

Be deferential in dealing with the world; deference is the starting line of progress. Be generous in your treatment of others; helping others is really the basis on which you help yourself.

Shame and disgrace should not be attributed completely to others but should be taken upon oneself as well, so as to conceal one's light and nourish virtue.

In whatever you do, if you leave a sense of incompleteness, then Creation cannot resent you, ghosts and spirits cannot harm you. If you insist on fulfillment in your work and perfection in achievement, you will become either inwardly deranged or outwardly unsettled.

Be pure yet tolerant, benevolent yet decisive, observant yet not intrusive, straightforward yet not stiff. As it is said, the best candy is not too sweet; the best seafood is not too salty.

If a poor house is well kept, or a poor girl well groomed, there is elegance if not beauty. If good people should come upon hard times, why should they immediately give up on themselves?

If you are not lax when at leisure, you will be effective when busy. If you are not absent-minded in tranquillity, that will be useful in action. If you are not hypocritical in private, that will show up in public.

When thoughts arise, as soon as you sense them heading on the road of desire, bring them right back onto the road of reason. Once they arise, notice them; once you notice them, you can change them. This is the key to turning calamity into fortune, rising from death and returning to life. Don't be careless and indulgent.

When your thoughts are perfectly clear in quietude, you see the real substance of the mind. When your mood is serene at leisure, you perceive the real workings of the mind.

When you are profoundly calm and aloof, you find the real taste of the mind. Nothing compares to these three ways of observing the mind and realizing enlightenment.

Calmness in quietude is not real calm; when you can be calm in the midst of activity, this is the true state of nature. Happiness in comfort is not real happiness; when you can be happy in the midst of hardship, then you see the true potential of the mind.

When you sacrifice yourself, do not hesitate; if you keep hesitating, your intention in sacrificing yourself will be disgraced. When you give to others, don't expect any reward; if you expect a reward, your intention in giving will be wrong.

When fate slights me in terms of prosperity, I respond by enriching my virtue. When fate belabors me physically, I make up for it by making my mind free. When fate obstructs me by circumstances, I get through by elevating my way of life. What can fate do to me?

Upright people have no thought of seeking prosperity; heaven then guides their sincerity through their innocence. Devious people are intent on avoiding misfortune; heaven then takes away their spirit through their obsession. So we can see the workings of heaven are most marvelous; human cleverness is helpless in this regard.

If a playgirl becomes a good wife in her later years, her early indiscretions don't matter. If a chaste wife loses her virtue in her later years, that cancels out her former purity. Truly it is well said, "When you observe people, just observe the second half of their lives."

If you want to know the bequest of your ancestors, it is what you are enjoying now. You should think about how hard it was to build this up. If you want to know about the welfare of your descendants, it is what you leave them. You should think about how easy it is to lose this.

If ordinary people will plant virtues and exercise generosity, they are nobles without rank. If grandees just hanker after power and sell favor, after all they become beggars with titles.

Gentlemen who feign goodness are no different from petty people who indulge in evil. Gentlemen who compromise their morals are not as good as lesser people who reform themselves.

When a family member has made a mistake, one should neither become enraged nor set it aside lightly. If something is hard to say, hint at it indirectly. If they do not understand today, admonish them again tomorrow. The model for family life is to be like the spring breeze melting ice.

If one sees complete fulfillment always in one's heart, there will be nothing defective in all the world. If the mind is kept open and equanimous, there will be no warped feelings in all the world.

People who are aloof will always be doubted by those who are obsessive. People who are strict will always be disliked by those who are indulgent. In such situations, enlightened people should never compromise their conduct, yet they should not reveal their sharpness too much either.

In adversity, everything that surrounds you is a kind of medicine that helps you refine your conduct, yet you are unaware of it. In pleasant situations, you are faced with weapons that will tear you apart, yet you do not realize it.

Those born and raised amid wealth and privilege have desires like a roaring fire, ambitions like fierce flames; if they do not keep some clarity and coolness, that fire and those flames will either burn other people or consume themselves.

Once people's hearts are genuine, they can affect the world positively. People who are false have no real self; they are detestable to others and a disgrace to themselves.

Culture at its best has nothing extraordinary, just what is appropriate. Personality at its best has nothing unusual, just what is natural.

In terms of ephemeral manifestations, even the body passes away, to say nothing of success, fame, wealth, and rank. In terms of reality, all beings are oneself, to say nothing of family members. If people can see through the ephemeral and recognize the real, then they can bear great social responsibilities and

臨流圖

at the same time be free from the bonds of the world.

Delicious foods are drugs that will inflame the gut and rot the bones, but there is no harm if one eats moderately. Delightful things are all purveyors of destruction and decadence, but there is no regret if one enjoys them moderately.

Do not criticize people for minor faults; do not reveal people's secrets; do not remember people's past wrongs. These three things can build character and prevent harm.

People should not take self-control lightly, because if they do, things can disturb them, and they have no sense of tranquil stability. People should not be obsessive in attending to affairs, because if they are, they will get bogged down by things and lack freedom and lively vigor.

The universe may exist indefinitely, but this body is not obtained a second time; human life only lasts a hundred years at most, and these days slip by easily. Those who would live happily know the joy of having life and remember the sorrow of wasting life.

Resentment becomes manifest because of goodwill; so rather than try to get people to exercise goodwill toward you, it is better to forget about both resentment and goodwill. Enmity is based on favor; so rather than try to get people's gratitude, it is better to forget about both enmity and favor.

The sicknesses of old age are brought on during one's youth; the troubles of one's declining years are created during one's prime. Therefore, people should be very careful when in full bloom.

Selling personal favor is not as good as assisting public consensus. Making new acquaintances is not as good as warming up old friendships. Establishing a glorious reputation is not as good as planting hidden virtues. Valuing unusual conduct is not as good as being careful about ordinary actions.

One should not oppose what is fair and just. If one does so, it will leave a legacy of shame. One should not enter in among power brokers. If ones does so, the stain will last all one's life.

Compromise to please others is not as good as integrity that annoys others. Rather than be praised without being good, it is better to be slandered without being bad.

When there is trouble among relatives, one should remain calm and not get excited. When friends are in error, one should be stern and not gloss over it lightly.

When one is not slipshod in small matters, not hypocritical in secret, and not reckless in disappointment, only then is one a true hero.

A thousand pieces of gold may hardly bring a moment's happiness, but a small favor can cause a lifetime's gratitude. Too much love can turn into enmity, while aloofness can produce joy.

Hide cleverness in clumsiness; act ignorant but be bright; use restraint to expand. These are three hiding places for dealing effectively with life.

Decline is inherent in prosperity, the potential for development is in destitution. So when at ease one should take care to think about trouble, and when in trouble one should be infinitely patient so as to eventually succeed.

Those who are amazed at wonders and delight in the extraordinary do not have great knowledge. Solitary ascetics do not have enduring discipline.

When anger or passion boils up, even when we are clearly aware we still go ahead. Who is it that is aware? Who is it that goes ahead? If we can turn our thoughts around in this way, the devil becomes the conscience.

Don't be biased in belief and let yourself be deceived by the dishonest. Don't rely on yourself too much and let yourself be compelled by moods. Don't use your own strengths to bring out others' shortcomings. Don't resent others' abilities on account of your own incompetence.

People's shortcomings should be treated with tact; if you expose them crudely, this is attacking weaknesses with a weakness. When people are stubborn, it requires skill to influence them; if you treat them with anger and spite, this is treating stubbornness with stubbornness.

When you meet silent and inscrutable people, don't tell them what you are thinking. When you meet irritable and self-serving people, be careful what you say.

When your thoughts are muddled or distracted, you should know how to alert yourself. When your thoughts are tense, you should know how to let them go. Otherwise, once you get rid of torpor you may bring on excitement.

A clear sunny day can suddenly shift to thunder and lightning, a raging storm can suddenly give way to a bright moonlit night. The weather may be inconstant, but the sky remains the same. The substance of the human mind should also be like this.

Regarding the work of self-mastery and control of desires, some say that if you do not perceive immediately, it will be hard to muster sufficient strength; some say that even with penetrating perception, forbearance is insufficient. Perception is a clear jewel that shows up demons; strength is a sword of wisdom that cuts down demons. Both are necessary.

To notice people's deceptions yet not reveal it in words, to bear people's insults without showing any change of attitude—there is endless meaning in this, and also endless function.

Unexpected hardship refines people; if you can accept it, both mind and body will benefit. If you cannot accept it, on the other hand, both mind and body will be harmed.

Our body is a small universe; to regulate emotions and feelings is a way of harmonization. The universe is a great set of parents; to cause people to be without enmity and things to be without affliction is a sign of warmth.

"One should have no intention to harm others, but should not lack the awareness to avoid being harmed by others." This is a warning against carelessness. "It is better to be deceived by people than to be on the lookout for deception." This is a warning against paranoia. If one can keep both of these sayings in mind, one can be precise and clear yet simple and friendly.

When parents are kind and children obedient, elder siblings friendly and younger siblings

白鷴

respectful, even if this is carried out to the fullest possible extent, it is all as it should be and is nothing to be considered impressive. If those who give are conscious of their own generosity and those who receive feel indebted, they are no longer family but rather strangers doing business.

When there is beauty, there is inevitably ugliness in contrast. If you do not take pride in your own beauty, who can consider you ugly? When there is purity, there must be defilement as its opposite. If you do not crave purity, who can defile you?

When it comes to changes of attitude, warm and cold, the rich are more extreme than the poor. When it comes to envy and resentment, relatives are worse than strangers. If you do not deal with such situations coolly and calmly, you will rarely avoid vexation.

Don't let the doubts of the crowd interfere with an individual view, but don't reject the words of others because of faith in your own opinion. Don't miss the larger reality by taking a little kindness personally; don't use public opinion to please yourself.

If you cannot become familiar with good people right away, it is not advisable to praise them beforehand, lest that incite slanderers. If you cannot easily get rid of bad people, it is not advisable to criticize them at first, lest that invite troublemakers.

Public behavior is nurtured in private; earth-shaking measures come from careful steps.

Merit and fault do not admit of the slightest mixup; if you mix them up, people will become lazy. Gratitude and enmity should not be too clear; if you make them too clear, people will be alienated.

When salary and rank are very great, there is danger. When skills are exerted to the utmost, there is decline. When manners are too dignified, there is criticism.

Darkness is bad for evil, light is bad for good. When evil is apparent, its harm is little; but when it is hidden its harm is great. When good is apparent, its merit is little; but when it is hidden its merit is great.

Virtue is the master of talent, talent is the servant of virtue. Talent without virtue is like a house where there is no master and the servant manages its affairs. How can there be no mischief?

To get rid of villains and knaves, it is necessary to give them a way out. If you don't give them any leeway at all, they will be like trapped rats. If every way out is closed to them, they will chew up everything good.

Share people's mistakes, but don't try to share in their achievements, for that will lead to resentment. Share people's troubles, but don't try to get a share of their happiness, for that will lead to enmity.

When enlightened people are so poor that they cannot help others, if they speak a word to awaken the confused or to resolve a problem, there is also boundless merit in that.

One of the common troubles of human sentiments is that people cleave to others when they are hungry and thus drift off when they are filled; they go to those who are in comfortable circumstances and abandon those who have fallen on hard times. Enlightened people should clarify their perception and see coolly, being careful to remain firm-hearted and not be easily shaken.

Virtue evolves according to capacity; capacity grows through perception. Therefore, if you would enrich your virtue, you must broaden your capacity; and if you would broaden your capacity, you must increase your perception.

When a lone lamp burns faintly and everything is silent, this is the time we enter quiet repose. When we have just awakened from dawn dreams and nothing is yet stirring, this is where we emerge from the undifferentiated. If you can take advantage of these moments to turn your attention around to inner awareness, then you will realize that senses and desires are all fetters.

For those who reflect on themselves, everything they encounter is medicine. For those who attack others, every thought is a weapon. One is the way to initiate all good, one is a way to deepen all evil. They are as far apart as sky and earth.

Business and scholarship pass away with the person, but the soul is forever like new. Fame and fortune change with the generations, but the spirit is always the same. Enlightened people surely should not exchange the lasting for the ephemeral.

A net set up to catch fish may snare a duck; a mantis hunting an insect may itself be set upon by a sparrow. Machinations are hidden within machinations; changes arise beyond changes. So how can wit and cleverness be relied upon?

If you are not at all truthful or sincere in your thoughts, you are useless to society, and everything you do is vain. If you have no roundness and liveliness in your way of life, you are a manikin and are inhibited every-where.

When water isn't rippled, it is naturally still. When a mirror isn't clouded, it is clear of itself. So the mind is not to be cleared; get rid of what muddles it, and its clarity will spontaneously appear. Pleasure need not be sought; get rid of what pains you, and pleasure is naturally there.

It is possible to transgress upon the taboo realm of ghosts and spirits with a single thought, to injure the harmony of heaven and earth with a single remark, and to brew trouble for your posterity with a single deed. Best beware.

There are some things that do not get cleared up by rushing them but may clarify themselves if given room to do so; in such cases, do not be hasty, lest that make people quick to anger. There are some people who are not made obedient by attempting to control them, but may civilize themselves if given the freedom to do so; in such cases, do not try to manipulate them rigorously, lest that increase their stubbornness.

Even if you have lofty ideals and write high-minded essays, if you do not form them by means of the essence of virtue, they will end up as personal mettle and spin-offs of technical ability.

When you retire from office, you should do so at the peak of your career. As for where to place yourself in society, you should live in the state of a survivor.

As you attend to your virtue, you should attend to it even in the minutest things. When you give charity, strive to give to those who cannot repay.

題壁圖

Association with city people is not as good as friendship with elderly peasants. Calling on upper-class mansions is not as good as getting to know peasant homes. Listening to the talk of the streets and alleys is not as good as hearing the songs of the woodcutters and shepherds. Talking about the moral failures and professional blunders of people today is not as good as retelling the fine words and noble deeds of people of old.

Your virtue is the foundation of your professional work; no house frame ever lasted without a solid foundation. Your mentality is the root of your prosperity; no branches and leaves ever flourished without a well-planted root.

One of our predecessors said, "Throwing away the inexhaustible treasury of your own home, you go with your bowl from door to door, acting like a beggar." He also said, "Let the poor who've made a windfall stop talking of dreams; in whose house has the hearth fire no smoke?" One saying cautions those who blind themselves to what they have; one cautions those who pride themselves in what they have. They can be taken as urgent warnings in the domain of education.

The Way is something public, into which people should be led according to the individual. Learning is an everyday affair, in which caution should be exercised in each situation.

Those who trust others will find that not everyone is necessarily sincere, but they will be sincere themselves. Those who suspect others will find that not everyone is necessarily deceiving them, but they have already become deceivers themselves.

Those who are broad-minded and considerate are like the spring breeze, warm and nurturing, at whose touch all beings grow. Those who are envious and cruel are like the snow of the northlands, stilling and freezing, at whose touch all beings die.

When you do good but do not see its benefit, it is like a squash growing in the grasses; it should naturally grow unknown. When you do evil but do not see its harm, it is like spring snow in the yard; it will inevitably sink in or evaporate.

When you meet old friends, your spirits should be all the more fresh. When you deal with private matters, your intentions should be all the more open. When you are treating people in their decline, your generosity and courtesy should be all the more magnanimous.

Diligence means to be keen in matters of virtue and justice, but worldly people use diligence to solve their economic difficulties. Frugality means to have little desire for material goods, but worldly people use frugality as a cover for stinginess. Thus do watchwords of enlightened life turn into tools for the private business of small people. What a pity!

Those who act on excitement act intermittently; this is hardly the way to avoid regression. Those whose understanding comes from emotional perceptions are as confused as they are enlightened; this is not a lamp that is constantly bright.

You should be forgiving when others make mistakes, but not when the mistakes are in you. You should be patient under duress yourself, but not when it affects others.

Generosity should begin lightly and deepen later, for when it is first rich and then lessens, people forget the kindness. Authority should begin strictly and loosen up later, for if it is loose first and then strict, people will resent the severity.

If you can be free of conventions, that is extraordinary; if you intentionally value the unusual, that is not extraordinary but weird. If you do not join the polluted, then you are pure; if you reject society in search of purity, that is not purity but fanaticism.

When the mind is empty, its essence appears. Trying to see the essence without stopping the mind is like stirring up waves looking for the moon. When the will is clean, the heart is pure. Seeking to clarify the heart without understanding the will is like obtaining a mirror and piling dust on it.

When you are in a high position and people serve you, they are serving your regalia of office. When you are in a humble position and people despise you, they are despising your simple attire. So since they are not serving you, why should you be glad? And since they are not despising you, why should you be angry?

"Always leave some food for the mice; pity the moths and don't light the lamp." Thoughts like these that the ancients had are the living, life-giving mechanism of us humans. Without this, we are no more than statues or manikins.

The substance of mind is the substance of heaven. A joyful thought is an auspicious star or a felicitous cloud. An angry thought is a thunderstorm or a violent rain. A kind thought is a gentle breeze or sweet dew. A stern thought is a fierce sun or an autumn frost. Which of these can be eliminated? Just let them pass away as they arise, open and unresisting, and your mind merges with the spacious sky.

When unoccupied, the mind is easily dimmed; best be very calm yet radiantly alert. When occupied, the mind easily runs wild; best be alert yet very calmly in control.

When people are in positions of power and occupy important offices, their behavior should be strict and clear, while their state of mind should be gentle and easy. Don't let a little accommodation bring you close to cliques of self-seekers; and don't let excessive intensity run you afoul of the poison of the vicious.

Those who make a show of morality are inevitably slandered on moral grounds; those who make a show of learning are always blamed on account of learning. Therefore, enlightened people neither approach evil nor establish a good repute. Only an integrated mood of harmony is of value in social life.

When you meet dishonest people, move them with sincerity. When you meet violent people, affect them with gentility. When you meet warped people, inspire them with justice. Then the whole world enters your forge.

A moment of kindness can produce a mood of harmony between heaven and earth. Purity of heart can leave a fine example for a hundred generations.

Hidden schemes, weird arts, strange practices, and unusual abilities are all sources of calamity in social and professional life. Only by normal qualities and normal actions can one keep natural wholeness and bring peace.

莉枝
此枝宜於薔薇
月季根下

There is a saying that goes, "Climbing a mountain, you endure steep pathways; walking in snow, you endure dangerous bridges." There is much meaning in the word "endure." For example, when dealing with unstable human feelings and uneven pathways in life, without endurance to hold you up, you may fall into a pit in the brush.

To boast of one's work or show off one's literary accomplishments is to base one's person on external things. People who do this do not know that the substance of mind is bright as it is, and as long as it is not lost, one may completely lack skills and learning yet still be a fine upstanding person.

If you would "snatch some leisure in the midst of hurry," you must first get a grip on it when you are already at leisure. If you would "grab some quiet in the midst of the hubbub," you must first establish self-mastery from quietude. Otherwise, anyone would be influenced by situations and over-whelmed by the course of events.

Don't obscure your own mind; don't exhaust people's emotions; don't use up material powers. With these three things, it is possible to establish a mind with universal perspective, establish meaningful ways of life for people in general, and create prosperity for descendants.

Here are two sayings for people in public office: "Only impartiality gives rise to clarity," and "Only honesty produces dignity." Here are two sayings for home life: "Only by forgiveness are feelings evened," and "Only by frugality are necessities sufficient."

When you are in positions of wealth and status, you should know the miseries of those who are poor and lowly. When you are young and strong, you should remember the pains of the old and feeble.

You should not be too much of a purist in your way of life, for you need to be able to accept all that is foul. You should not be too clear in making distinctions in social interactions, for you need to accept everyone whether they are good or bad, wise or foolish.

Give up antagonism to small people, for small people have their own peers. Give up trying to flatter and charm enlightened people, for enlightened people don't do personal favors.

The sickness of indulging desires can be treated, but the sickness of clinging to abstract principles is hard to treat. Obstacles presented by events and objects can be removed, but obstacles presented by social principles are hard to remove.

Polish what you polish until it is like gold that has been refined a hundred times; anything that is done in a hurry is not deeply developed. Do what you do like a thousand-pound catapult; one who pops off too easily does not accomplish much.

It is better to be reviled by petty people than to be flattered by them. It is better to be rebuked by enlightened people than to be indulged by them.

When those who like to gain something for themselves exceed the bounds of reason and right, the harm is obvious and therefore shallow. When those who are interested in their own reputation weasel their way into reason and right, the harm is hidden and therefore deep.

To accept people's favors yet not repay them no matter how serious they are, to take revenge on those with whom you have any grievances no matter how slight they are, to give credence to anything bad you hear about others even if it is not evident, to doubt whatever good you hear even if it is obvious: this is all extremely cruel and heartless. Best beware.

Cavilers and calumniators are like flecks of cloud temporarily blocking the sun; it will be clear again before long. Flatterers and fawners are like a draft that gets into the flesh; one is harmed unawares.

There are no trees on the high mountain crags; plants and trees grow in profusion in the valley bowls. There are no fish in the rapids; fish and turtles gather in the still depths. Thus, enlightened people are wary of impractical actions and fanatical attitudes.

Most people who are successful in their work are open-minded and well rounded. Those who fail in their undertakings and lose opportunities are the obstinate and inflexible.

In social life, it is not good to be a conformist, yet it is not good to be a nonconformist either. In doing things, it is not good to cause people aversion, yet it is not good to try to gain their favor either.

At dusk the sunset is beautifully bright; at year's end the tangerines are even more fragrant. Therefore, at the end of their road, in their later years, enlightened people should be a hundred times more vital in spirit.

A hawk stands as though dozing, a tiger walks as though ill; these are ploys by which they claw and bite. So enlightened people should not show their brilliance and talent, for only thus have they the power to bear great responsibilities.

Frugality is an excellent quality, but if excessive it becomes stinginess and miserliness, which instead damage the good life. Deference is fine conduct, but if excessive it becomes servility and cautiousness, which often come from a scheming mind.

Don't worry about what offends you; don't take a liking to what pleases you. Don't count on a prolonged state of ease; don't shrink in fear at the first difficulty.

Those who drink and party are not good neighbors. Those who are addicted to vanities of repute are not good citizens. Those who think much of fame and status are not good public officials.

Worldly people enjoy what agrees with them, then are pulled by enjoyment into misery. Enlightened people enjoy what offends them, as ultimately they gain happiness for their pains.

Those who dwell in fullness are like water about to overflow; don't add another drop. Those who are in urgent danger are like wood that is about to snap; don't add any more pressure.

Observe people with cool eyes, listen to their words with cool ears. Confront feelings with cool emotions, reflect on principles with a cool mind.

Humane people are broad-minded, so they are richly blessed and have lasting happiness; everything they do makes an atmosphere of relaxation. Base men are fussy, so they are less fortunate and their good times are short; everything they do is a model of fussiness.

于久畫泉法

When you hear of bad people, don't despise them right away, for their bad repute might be the sputterings of cavilers. When you hear of good people, don't rush to befriend them, because their good repute might have been made up by dishonest people trying to get ahead.

The reckless and crude-minded accomplish nothing whatever. To those who are gentle-hearted and even-minded, a hundred blessings accrue of themselves.

When you employ people, don't be harsh, for if you are harsh, even the earnest workers will leave. When you make friends, it is not good to be promiscuous, for if you are promiscuous, then flatterers will come to you.

In a blasting wind and driving rain, it is necessary to stand fast. In the midst of finery and glamour, it is necessary to set one's sights on high. Where the road is perilous and the pathway steep, it is necessary to turn back early.

If conservative and moralistic people complement this with harmony and balance, only then will they avoid anger and contention. If successful and famous people bear this with modesty and virtue, only then will they avoid inspiring envy and jealousy.

When prominent people are in public office, they should not write letters without restraint. It is necessary to be inscrutable to others, to prevent opportunists from taking advantage. When in private life, on the other hand, it will not do to be remote and aloof. It is essential to be easily visible to others, to deepen old friendships.

You should fear important people, for if you do so, you will not be heedless. You should also fear small people, for if you do so, you will not be known for acting like a thug.

When things are not going your way, then think of those who are worse off than you, and resentment will naturally disappear. When your mind lazes off, then think of those who are better than you, and your vital spirit will be naturally aroused.

Don't get so carried away by delight that you agree too easily; don't get so drunk that you give rise to anger. Don't get so high-spirited that you take on too many things; don't let fatigue reduce your achievements.

To be good at reading the classics, you must read to the point where your hands and feet dance, for only thus do you avoid getting caught in literalism. To be good at observing things, you must observe to the point where your mind merges with them, for only thus do you avoid getting mired in the forms they leave behind.

Heaven makes individuals intelligent so that they may instruct the ignorant, but in society those individuals flaunt their talents to show up people's shortcomings. Heaven enriches individuals so that they may help the destitute, but in society those individuals cling to their possessions to lord over the poor. Such individuals are truly capital criminals against heaven.

Complete people have no thoughts or worries, while ignorant people have no knowledge; both can be partners in study or business. It is only the mediocre intellectuals who think too much and have too much information, so that they also do too much thinking and doubting; as a result it is hard to do anything at all with them.

Speech is the gate of the heart; if you do not guard your speech closely, you divulge all the real workings of your mind. Attention is the mind's feet; if you do not control your attention strictly, it runs into misleading pathways.

When you take others to task, if you look for where they are faultless in spite of having other faults, then feelings will be equanimous. When you take yourself to task, if you look for where there are flaws in your impeccability, then virtue will progress.

Children are embryos of adults; intellectuals are embryos of grandees. If the power of the development process at that time is not complete and the molding is impure, on another day, when they are members of society and government officials, it will turn out to be virtually impossible for them to function well.

Enlightened people in trouble still do not worry, yet in merriment are still cautious. They are not cowed when they meet socially prominent people, but they are moved by the plight of the orphaned.

Although peach and plum blossoms are beautiful, how do they compare with the constancy of the green in the pine and cedar? Although pears and apricots are sweet, how do they compare with the intensely fragrant coolness of the oranges and tangerines? How true it is that a short life of luxury is not as good as a simple life that is long, that early blooming and fruitage are not as good as late perfection.

When the wind is still and the waves are quiet, you see the true realm of human life. When flavor is light and sound is rare, you know the original state of the body of mind.

Those who talk about the pleasures of mountains and forests have not necessarily really attained the pleasures of mountains and forests. Those who disdain talk of fame and fortune have not necessarily completely forgotten feelings for fame and fortune.

Fishing is just a pastime, but even so one holds the handle of life and death. Chess is just a game, but even so it stirs the warlike mind. Obviously, it is more comfortable to minimize occupations than to avidly seek them; and it is more wholesome to be simple than to be clever.

When nightingales and flowers are abundant and the mountains and valleys are steeped in luxuriant beauty, this is all an illusory state of heaven and earth. When the waters dry, the leaves fall, the rocks are bared, and the cliffs withered, then you see the real self of heaven and earth.

The months and years are originally long, but people in a hurry themselves shorten them. Heaven and earth are originally wide, but base people make them narrow. The four seasons are originally serene, but people who fuss and worry make them a bother.

It doesn't take much for some atmosphere—a bit of haze and mist over a little pond and a few rocks, and that's enough. One needn't go far for scenery—the breeze and the moon at a rustic window are naturally serene.

Listening to the sound of a bell on a still night awakens one from a dream in a dream;

素問圖

watching the reflection of the moon in a clear pool, one espies a body beyond the body.

The speech of the birds and the voices of the insects are all the secret of transmitting mind; the brilliance of the flowers and colors of the grasses are all writings on seeing the Way. To learn, it is necessary to have your higher potential clarified thoroughly and your heart clear as crystal. Then you will find understanding of mind whatever you encounter.

People know how to read books with writing in them, but they do not know how to read unwritten books. They know how to play a harp with strings, but they do not know how to play a stringless harp. If you work through traces and not through spirit, how can you get the aim of music and literature?

When there are no material desires in the mind, it is like a clear sea under the autumn sky. If you have a harp and some books at your side, they make an immortal abode in a mountain fastness.

When guests and friends gather in great numbers and drink heavily, they enjoy themselves with abandon. Suddenly, the night is spent, the candles burn low; the incense is gone, the tea is cold. Unawares, people find themselves gagging and choking, making them feel desolate and taking away the fun. Just about everything in the world is like this, so why don't people wake up sooner?

When you understand the sense of the here and now, the misty moonlight of the scenic lakes will all enter your heart. When you break through the machinations before your eyes, the heroics of the ages will all wind up in the palm of your hand.

Mountains, rivers, and continents are already just atoms, and we are but particles within those atoms. The physical body will presently turn out to be a bubble, a shadow, and so will all the other shadows outside your shadow. If you do not have the highest knowledge, you do not have the clearest mind.

Life passes by in a flash, yet people vie and compete with each other. How much time do we have? There is very little room, yet people contest and debate with each other. How big is the world?

A cold lamp without flame, a worn leather coat without warmth—both are but shadows of themselves. Similarly, if your body is like a withered tree and your mind is like dead ashes, you unavoidably fall into stupid vacantness.

If people are willing to stop at once, then they finish at once. If you insist on seeking a place of rest, then "even though you've married off all your children, there are no fewer things to do; even though monkhood is fine, you still haven't understood your heart." An ancient said, "If you stop now, then stop; if you seek an ending, there is no ending." This is highly perceptive.

When you look upon fervor from coolness, then you know the vanity of frenetic activity in fervor. When you enter from hurry into leisure, then you notice how the flavor in quietude lasts longest.

There is a way to look upon wealth and status as like floating clouds without having to live in a mountain cave. One need not be addicted to springs and rocks to be always drinking by oneself and lost in poetry.

Let people compete if they will, but do not despise them for all being intoxicated. Be calm and aloof to suit yourself, but do not be proud of being the only one who is sober. This is what Buddhists call not being bound by religion, not being bound by voidness, body and mind both free.

Length and brevity of time depend on a thought; breadth or narrowness of space depend on the heart. So for one whose mind is free, a day is longer than a thousand ages; for one whose mind is broad, a small room is wider than heaven and earth.

Whatever meets the eye is the realm of immortals for the contented, the realm of mortals for the discontented. All the bases of activity in society have life-giving potential if used well and death-dealing potential if not used well.

The calamities brought about by cleaving to the powerful are very severe, and also very swift. The savor of a simple life is most delicate, and most enduring.

I walk alone with my staff by a valley stream among the pines; where I stand, clouds rise about my ragged patchwork robe. I sleep aloof with a book for my pillow under a window framed with bamboo; when I wake, the moon's gotten into the worn felt.

Sexual desire may burn like fire, but when you give a thought to when you are ill, then your excitement dies down. Fame and fortune may be as sweet as candy, but when you give a thought to when you die, then their flavor is like chewing wax. Therefore, if people are usually concerned about death and illness, this can also dissolve unreal activities and develop longing for the Way.

The road of contention for precedence is narrow; take a step back, and it broadens a step. The rich flavor of intense beauty is short-lived; dilute it with a measure of pure clarity, and it will naturally last that much longer.

If you will have your nature undisturbed in busy situations, it is necessary that mind and spirit be nurtured to pure clarity when at leisure.

In the forest of hidden aloofness, there is neither glory nor disgrace. On the road of enlightened justice, there is neither heat nor cool.

Even if you can't get rid of the heat, as long as you can get rid of bother with the heat, your body is always on a cool terrace. Even if you can't get rid of poverty, as long as you can get rid of the sadness of poverty, your mind always lives in a comfortable abode.

If you immediately think about stepping back whenever you step ahead, you may avoid the calamity of bumping into fences. If you plan to detach yourself beforehand whenever you start a project, only then will you escape the danger of mounting a tiger.

When greedy people are given gold, they are bitter that they haven't gotten jewels; when they are made barons they are resentful that they haven't been made lords. Though powerful and rich, their attitude is that of beggars. For those who know how to be content, simple fare is more delicious than rich delicacies, a cloth coat is warmer than fox fur, and an ordinary citizen does not defer to a king or a lord.

Taking pride in fame is not as interesting as avoiding it. Cultivating hobbies is not as peaceful as minimizing interests.

Those who enjoy silence understand mysteries as they watch white clouds and recondite

畫江海

rocks. Those who head for glory forget weariness when they see fine singing and dancing. Only for those who are masters of themselves is there no noise or silence, no flourishing or withering, nowhere that is not a spontaneously comfortable heaven.

A lone cloud emerges from a mountain cave, with nothing at all to keep it from going or staying. A bright mirror hangs in the sky, unaffected by either quiet or uproar.

The sense of eternity is found not in fine wine but in eating beans and drinking water. The mood of lament comes not from loneliness but from flutes and harps. So we know that the flavor of intense experience is always short-lived, while the charm of subtle experience alone is real.

Chan Buddhism says, "When hungry eat, when tired sleep." A work on the essence of poetry says, "The scene before the eyes is expressed in everyday sayings." Generally speaking, that which is most lofty dwells in that which is most ordinary; that which is most difficult emerges from that which is most easy. Those with subjective ideas are farthest away, while those who are mindless are naturally close.

When there is no sound even as the stream flows, you are able to perceive the mood of quiet in the midst of clamor. When the clouds are unobstructed in spite of the height of the mountains, you realize the way to leave being and enter nonbeing.

Mountain forests are beautiful places, but once you become attached to them, they become cities. Calligraphy and painting are elegant pastimes, but once you get greedy they become commercialized. In general, when the mind is unattached, then the realm of desire is the capital of immortals; when the mind is attached, then objects of pleasure become an ocean of suffering.

The way to transcend the world is right in the midst of involvement with the world; it is not necessary to cut off human relations to escape society. The work of understanding the mind is right in the midst of full use of the mind; it is not necessary to exterminate desire to make the mind like ashes.

Always put yourself in a position where there is room; then who can manipulate you by glory or disgrace, gain or loss? Always rest your mind in tranquillity; then who can fool you about right and wrong or advantage and disadvantage?

If I do not seek prosperity, how can I be bothered by the fragrant bait of profitable emolument? If I do not compete to get ahead, why should I fear the crises of officialdom?

In times of clamor and confusion, one tends to forget what one ordinarily remembers in a state of clarity and calm, one tends to glimpse what one had forgotten long ago. So we can see that as soon as stillness and business are divided, darkness and light suddenly diverge.

Lying in the snow, sleeping in the clouds, under a reed-flower quilt, I keep a room of night breath whole. In a cup of wine I sing with the breeze, enjoying the moon, having sidestepped tidal waves of red dust.

When an entourage of aristocrats includes a mountain man, it has a more lofty air. When a leather-clothed courtier is on a road traveled by fisherfolk and woodcutters, it adds so much vulgarity. So we know that richness is not superior to austerity, vulgarity is not as good as refinement.

When you roam in the mountain forests, among the springs and rocks, the materialistic mentality gradually ceases. When you steep yourself in poetry, writing, and painting, the mood of worldliness fades away. So even though enlightened people do not amuse themselves with objects to the point where they lose their will, yet they ordinarily use the environment as a means of tuning the mind.

The atmosphere of spring makes people's hearts and spirits relax, but that is not as good as the white of the clouds and clarity of the wind in autumn, the fragrance of the orchids and cassia, the water and sky one color, above and below empty and bright, making people's spirits and bones both pure.

Those who have poetic ideas even though they are illiterate attain the true enjoyment of poets. Those who have the taste of Chan even though they haven't studied it understand the mysterious devices of Chan Buddhism.

When the workings of the mind are stirred, a reflection of a bow may be mistaken for a serpent, a large rock in the underbrush may be seen as a crouching lion; here is all killing energy. When thoughts cease, even the violent can become gentle, the ordinary can be elegant; everywhere you see true potential.

When the body is like an unmoored boat, it may go with the flow or come to a stop. When the mind is like wood reduced to ashes, what does it matter whether one is cut by swords or painted with perfume?

To delight in listening to the call of the nightingale, to weary of hearing the croaking of frogs, to want to cultivate flowers on seeing them, to wish to remove weeds on finding them: these are human sentiments, and this is just acting on form and mood. If you look upon beings in terms of the essential creative power in them, are they not all spontaneously expressing their natural potential and sense of aliveness?

When your hair falls out and you lose your teeth, you let the chiseling and fading of the illusory form go. When the birds sing and the flowers bloom, you know the real likeness of inherent nature.

If you fill your heart with desires, waves boil even on a cold pool, and you do not experience tranquillity even if you are in a mountain forest. If you empty your heart, coolness arises even in scorching heat, and you do not notice the hubbub even if you are in a city.

The more people possess, the greater their losses; so the rich are not as carefree as the poor. The higher people rise, the faster they fall, so the upper classes are not as secure as the common people.

It is just because people take themselves too seriously that they develop all sorts of addictions and passions. An ancient said, "If you do not even recognize the existence of self, how can you recognize value in things?" Also, "If you know the body is not the self, how can passions afflict you?" These sayings really hit the target.

Looking upon youth from the perspective of old age can melt away ambition and contentiousness. Looking upon success from the point of view of dereliction can stop thoughts of glamour.

Human feelings and social conditions are very mercurial and should not be taken too seriously. A philosopher said, "What you called your self before is now already another. I wonder who today's self will belong to later?" If people make this observation from time to time, they can unclog their hearts.

Open a cool eye in the midst of intense activity, and you save yourself that much bitter thought. Keep an enthusiastic attitude in hard times, and you gain that much true enjoyment.

When there is a pleasant state, there is an unpleasant state in contrast. When there is a good situation, there is one that is not good to replace it. Only an ordinary, simple life is a comfortable nest.

If you know that whatever is made inevitably breaks down, you needn't seek too hard for achievement. If you know that all living beings inevitably die, you needn't work too hard on health lore.

An ancient saint said, "As bamboo shadows sweep the stairs, no dust is stirred; as the moonlight penetrates the pond, no ripple is made on the water." A Confucian said, "Rapid as the flow of the river may be, the surroundings are always calm; though the flowers fall again and again, the mood is naturally relaxed." If people can keep these attitudes to deal with events and interact with others, how free they are in body and mind!

The rhymes of the pines in the forest, the murmuring of a spring in the rocks—listen to them in quietude, and you know the natural music of sky and earth. The glow of mist in the meadows, the reflections of clouds in the river—gaze on them calmly, and you see the highest art of the universe.

Even if people see wastelands in the wake of war, they still take pride in their weapons. Even though people are to be eaten by the animals of the graveyards, they still cling to material goods. There is a saying that goes, "It is easier to tame wild beasts than to conquer the human mind; it is easier to fill up a canyon than to satisfy the human mind."

When there are no wind and waves in your mind, then wherever you are is all green mountains and trees. When there is evolutionary development in your nature, then everywhere you go you see fish leap and birds fly.

As fish dart through water, they are forgetful of the water; as birds fly on the breeze, they are not conscious that there is a breeze. Discern this, and you can transcend the burden of things and enjoy natural potential.

Foxes sleep on broken steps, rabbits run on overgrown terraces; all are former sites of song and dance. Dew lies cold on yellow flowers, mist meanders through wilting grasses; all are old battlegrounds of past wars. Where is there any constancy in flourishing and decline? Where are the strong and the weak? It cools people's minds down to think of this.

Undisturbed by favor or disgrace, at leisure I watch the flowers in the garden bloom and then drop. With no intention of either going or staying, casually I follow the receding and spreading of the clouds.

In a clear sky with a bright moon, what heaven cannot be roamed in flight? Yet the moths cast themselves into the night lamplight. Where there are pure springs and green grass, what creatures cannot eat and drink? Yet the owls like rotting rats. How many people in the world are there who do not act like moths or owls?

Only those who think of giving up a raft as soon as they have gotten on it are really unobsessed wayfarers. Those who mount an ass and then go looking for an ass turn out to be unenlightened meditation instructors.

The powerful and prominent soar like dragons, the heroic and valiant fight like tigers:

but if you look upon them with cool eyes, they are like ants gathering on rancid meat, like flies swarming on blood. Judgments of right and wrong arise like hornets, gain and loss bristle like porcupine quills: but if you meet them with cool feelings, that is like a forge melting metal, like hot water dissolving snow.

When you are fettered by material desires, you feel that your life is pathetic; but when you immerse yourself in essential reality, you feel that your life is enjoyable. When you know life is pathetic, material senses are immediately seen through; when you know life is enjoyable, the realm of sages comes of itself.

When there are no longer any material desires in your heart, they are like snow melted in the flames of a furnace, like ice melted in the sun. When there is a single open clarity spontaneously before your eyes, then you see that the moon is in the blue sky and its reflection is in the waves.

What has been kept down for a long time will surely soar to the heights when it flies. What has bloomed first will be the soonest to fade. If you know this, you can avoid the trouble of becoming worn out on the way, and you can dissolve thoughts of impulsive hurry.

When deciduous trees go bare, then you know the vain glory of flowers and leaves; when people are sealed in their coffins, you know that children and wealth are no help.

True emptiness is not empty; clinging to appearances is not reality, nor is denying appearances. How did Buddha communicate this? "Be in the world, yet beyond the world." Pursuing desires is painful, but so is stopping desire altogether. It is up to us to cultivate ourselves skillfully.

A just person will defer a whole state, a greedy person will fight over a coin. Their personalities are vastly different, yet fondness for honor is no different from fondness for gain. An emperor runs a country, a beggar cries for a meal. Their ranks are vastly different, but how is feverish thinking different from feverish talking?

When you've had your fill of the flavors of the world and know them intimately, then whatever may happen, you are not terribly concerned. When you understand human feelings completely, then whatever people may call you, you just nod.

People today concentrate on the quest to have no thoughts but find that their thoughts ultimately cannot be annihilated. Just don't linger on the preceding thought, don't greet the following thought; if you can just use the present adaptation to circumstances to break through, you will naturally enter nothingness in a gradual manner.

Whatever spontaneously occurs to your mind is fine. When things come out naturally, only then do you see their real potential. If you add any adjustment or arrangement, grace is lost. One of the immortal poets said, "The

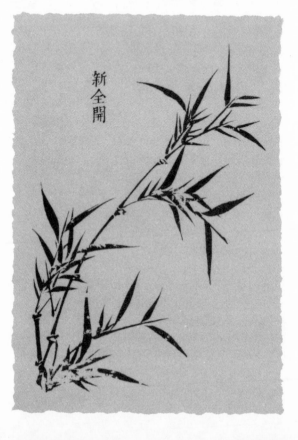

mind is comfortable whenever free of concerns; the breeze is clear as it blows along with nature."

When your essential nature is thoroughly pure, then even eating when hungry and drinking when thirsty strengthen and help body and mind. When your mind is sunk in confusion, even if you talk about meditation and expound verses, all of it is mental gymnastics.

There is a real state in the human mind that is naturally calm and pleasant even without music, naturally clear and fragrant even without incense and tea. You can swim in it only when the mind is clean and objects are empty, when worries are forgotten and the body is at ease.

Gold comes from ore, jade comes from stone. If not for illusion, there would be no way to seek reality. The Way is found in wine, immortals are met among the flowers. Even if refined, one cannot leave the ordinary world.

The myriad beings in sky and earth, the myriad feelings in human relations, the myriad affairs of the social world: when you look upon them with the ordinary eye, they are each different; but when you look upon them with the eye of the Way, all of them are normal. Why bother to discriminate? What's the use of grasping and rejecting?

When the spirit is ecstatic, one finds the mellowing energy of heaven and earth even in humble circumstances. When you savor things to the full, after simple fare you know the reality of plainness in human life.

Whether you are bound up or free is all in your own mind. When the mind is perfectly understood, even the profane world is a pure land as it is. Otherwise, even if you take up classical culture and have elegant hobbies, bedevilments are still there. It is said, "If you can stop, the realms of the senses become the realm of reality. If you don't understand, you are a worldling, even if a priest." How true!

When you suddenly hear a bird warbling in the midst of utter silence, it calls up so many mysterious feelings. When you suddenly see a lone branch bearing a flower after all the plants have withered away, it touches off un-limited living potential. So it can be seen that the sky of nature never withers permanently, and the spirit of potential is best touched off.

One poet said, "Better let body and mind be free, tacitly leaving them up to Creation." Another said, "Better collect body and mind, stabilize them, and return them to tranquil poise." Now "letting be free" can deteriorate into wildness, while "collecting" can get into quietism. Only those who skillfully control body and mind, and who can deliberately exercise mastery, can collect and let free autonomously.

On a winter night when the land is covered with snow and the moon is in the sky, your state of mind is clarified simply and spontaneously. When you feel the gentle energy of the spring breeze, your psychological realm is also naturally harmonized. Creation and the human mind merge intimately without separation.

Those who turn things around by themselves do not rejoice at gain or grieve over loss; the whole world is the range they roam. Those who are themselves used by things hate it when events go against them and love it when they go their way; the slightest thing can create binding entanglements.

When reason is calm, things are calm, so to avoid things in order to hold to reason is like trying to get rid of the shadow but keep the form. When mind is empty, objects are empty, so to keep away from objects in order to maintain the mind is like shooing away insects while gathering raw meat.

Try to think of what you were like before you were born, and also what you will be like after you die. Then myriad thoughts cool down, leaving your whole essence calm; you are thus spontaneously able to transcend things and live in a state prior to formalization.

If you treasure strength only after having gotten sick, or value peace only after having experienced turmoil, that is not being quick-witted. If you run into good fortune but realize already that it can be the basis of calamity, or if in your eagerness for life you realize beforehand that it is the cause of death, that would seem to be a lofty view.

Performers put on makeup and portray beauty and ugliness; but when the play is over, where are beauty and ugliness then? Chess players vie for precedence and seek to better each other in their moves; but when the game is over and the pieces are put away, where is the contest then?

When mind is mindless, what is there to contemplate? When Buddhists talk about contemplating mind, they increase their obstacles. Things are originally one thing; what need have they of equalization? When Taoists talk about equalizing things, they themselves split their sameness.

As long as your self-mastery is uncertain, it is best to be aloof of the mundane world, causing the mind not to see anything desirable and so not to be disturbed, thus to clarify your state of tranquillity. Once your discipline is firm, you should get involved in the mundane world again, causing the mind not to be disturbed even on seeing desirable things, thus to nurture your rounded capacity.

Those who like tranquillity and dislike clamor tend to avoid people to seek quietude. They do not know that when one wishes there were no one around, that is egotism; and when the mind is attached to quietude, that is the root of disturbance. How can they reach the state where others and oneself are seen as one, where disturbance and quietude are both forgotten?

When I get into a happy mood and walk barefoot in the fragrant grass, sometimes wild birds forget their wariness and accompany me. When the scenery suits my mind and I open my collar and sit still under falling flowers, white clouds slowly gather without saying a word.

The realms of good fortune and calamity in human life are all made of thoughts and imaginings. Therefore Buddhists say that the burning of desire for gain is itself a pit of fire, while drowning in greedy love is itself a bitter sea. The moment thoughts are pure, fierce flames become a pond; the moment you become aware, the boat has arrived on the further shore. If your thoughts vary at all, your world will immediately differ; so can we not be careful?

Chafing rope can cut through wood, dripping water can pierce stone; those who study the Way need to seek it with extra effort. Where water reaches a channel forms, when a melon is ripe the stem falls off; those who attain the Way entrust everything to the workings of nature.

雷隠公翁

When machinations cease, then the moon is there and the breeze comes; so one needn't experience the world as an ocean of misery. When the mind is aloof, there are no dust and tracks from the rat race; so why get addicted to mountains?

As soon as the plants and trees have withered, they show sprouts at the roots. Even though the order of the seasons brings freezing cold, eventually it brings back sunny energy. In the midst of purging and killing, the sense of continually renewing life is always in control. Thereby one can see the heart of heaven and earth.

When you gaze on the colors of the mountains after a rain, the scenery seems freshly beautiful. When you listen to the sound of a

bell on a still night, the tone is most sub-
limely clear.

Climbing a high mountain makes people's
hearts broad; gazing into a stream makes
people's minds aloof. Reading books on a
rainy or snowy night makes people's spirits
clear; relaxing and humming a tune on top of
a knoll makes people's feelings soar.

Without the wind and moon, flowers and
willows, there wouldn't be Creation; without
sensual desires and likings, there wouldn't be
the substance of mind. As long as you oper-
ate things by yourself and do not let things
use you, then likes and desires are all celestial
mechanisms, senses and feelings are themselves the realm of principle.

When you understand yourself as an individual, only then can you entrust all things to all things. When you return the world to the world, only then can you transcend the mundane while in the mundane.

If a person's life is too leisurely, extraneous thoughts arise insidiously; but if one is too busy, true essence does not appear. Therefore, enlightened people should not fail to embrace the concerns of body and mind, yet they still should not fail to steep themselves in aesthetic delights.

The human mind often loses reality through movement. If you sit in a state of clear serenity without a single thought born, then as clouds arise, you calmly go off into the distance with them; as raindrops patter, you coolly share in their purity. As the birds call, you joyfully sense communication; as flowers fall, you have a profound understanding of yourself. Where is not the realm of reality, what is not the working of reality?

When a child is born, the mother is endangered; when money piles up, robbers look in: so what joy is not a worry? When you are poor, you are willing to economize; if you are sick you are willing to take care of your body: so what worry is not a joy? Therefore, people of attainment should look upon ups and downs as one, and let both joy and sorrow be forgotten.

When the ear is like a valley, through which whirlwinds pass casting echoes, letting them go through and not keeping them, then "right" and "wrong" both disappear. When the mind is like a pond reflecting the moon, open and unattached to the forms in it, then things and self are both forgotten.

When worldly people get tangled and bound by prestige and profit, they are apt to call the material world a sea of misery. They are not aware of the white of the clouds or the green of the mountains, the flow of the river or the lay of the rocks, the response of the valleys to the songs of the woodcutters. The world is not material, the sea of life is not misery— they just make their own minds materialistic and miserable.

Flowers should be viewed when half open, wine should be drunk only to subtle intoxication; there is great fun in this. If you view

flowers in full bloom and drink to drunken-
ness, it becomes a bad experience. Those
who are living to the full should think about
this.

Wild vegetables are not irrigated by people,
wild animals are not raised by people; their
taste is flavorful and clear. If we can avoid
being stained by things of the world, will our
smell not be vastly different?

If you are going to raise flowers, grow bamboo, enjoy the birds, and watch fish, you do
need to have some self-mastery. If you are
just passing the time as a sightseer or aes-
thete, this is what Confucians call superfici-
ality and what Buddhists call insensitive
openness. What refined sense is there in that?

Educated people who live in the mountains and forests are poor because of their high ethical standards, but the delights of freedom are plenty in themselves. Farmers in the fields lead rustic and simple lives, but their natural reality is all there. If you might lose yourself to merchants in the cities, it would be better to fall and die in a ditch or a ravine with your spirit and character still clean.

Fortune you don't deserve and gains gotten for no reason are either Creation's hook and bait or traps of the human world. If your perception is not highly developed here, you will rarely avoid falling for their devices.

Human life is like a puppet. Just keep the root and stem in hand, so that not a single string gets tangled up, and you can reel in and reel out freely, action and response being up to you, not subject to the slightest control by anyone else Then you transcend this stage play.

When something happens, some harm is done. This is why everyone usually considers it lucky when life is uneventful. I read a poem by someone who lived in the past that said, "I urge you not to talk about the affairs of entitlement as a lord; for a single general's success, ten thousand skeletons dry in the sun." Also, "If everything were always peaceful, swords might well rust in their scabbards for a thousand years." Even though I had a heroic heart and a fierce spirit, unawares they turned to ice and hail.

Promiscuous women may become nuns to feign reform, while obsessive men may enter religion due to some stimulus or excitement. This is why the "schools of clear purity" are always hotbeds of promiscuous and perverted people.

The people in a boat on rough water don't know to fear, while bystanders are frozen with terror; the people in a group being reviled by a madman do not know to be alarmed, while onlookers bite their tongues. Therefore, enlightened people may be physically in the world, but their minds must transcend the world.

Human life is made freer by minimization. For example, if you party less, you avoid that much more frenzy, and if you speak less, you avoid that much more resentment. If you think less, your vital spirit doesn't get worn

鶴

out, and if you are less clever, your wholeness can be preserved. Those who seek not to lessen daily but to increase daily are really fettering their lives.

The cold and heat of the climate are easy to avoid, compared with the difficulty of eliminating the fevers and chills of human society. But the fevers and chills of human society are easy to eliminate, compared with the difficulty of getting rid of the ice and embers in one's mind. If you can get rid of the ice and embers inside you, your whole body will be filled with harmonious energy and the spring breeze will naturally be there wherever you are.

The Buddhist teaching of adapting to conditions and the Confucian teaching of plain living are rafts to cross the ocean. This is because the ways of the world are uncertain, and a single thought of seeking to have everything leads to myriad complications. If you make yourself comfortable wherever you happen to be, you can go anywhere.

## About the Illustrations

The illustrations presented with the text were selected from two well-known Chinese collections originally published in the seventeenth century: *Chieh-tzu-yüan hua chuan* (known as "The Mustard Seed Garden Manual of Painting"), and *San-ts'ai t'u-hui* (portions of which appeared in *Heaven and Earth: Album Leaves from a Ming Encyclopedia*, selected and annotated by John A. Goodall, 1979).